First World War
and Army of Occupation
War Diary
France, Belgium and Germany

56 DIVISION
Divisional Troops
280 Brigade Royal Field Artillery
21 March 1916 - 31 May 1916

WO95/2940/2

The Naval & Military Press Ltd
www.nmarchive.com
Published in association with The National Archives

Published by

The Naval & Military Press Ltd

Unit 10 Ridgewood Industrial Park,

Uckfield, East Sussex,

TN22 5QE England

Tel: +44 (0) 1825 749494

www.naval-military-press.com

www.nmarchive.com

This diary has been reprinted in facsimile from the original. Any imperfections are inevitably reproduced and the quality may fall short of modern type and cartographic standards.

© **Crown Copyright**
Images reproduced by permission of The National Archives, London, England, 2015.

Contents

Document type	Place/Title	Date From	Date To
Heading	WO95/2940/1		
Heading	56th Division 'B' Sqdn 2nd King Ed's Horse Mar-May 1916		
Heading	56th Divisional Cavalry 'B" Squadron 2nd King Edward's Horse 21st To 31st March 1916		
War Diary		21/03/1916	23/03/1916
War Diary	Grand Rullecourt	24/03/1916	31/03/1916
Heading	56th Divisional Cavalry "B" Squadron 2nd King Edward's Horse April 1916		
War Diary	Grand Rullecourt	01/04/1916	30/04/1916
Miscellaneous	D.A.G. 3rd Echelon	01/05/1916	01/05/1916
Heading	56th Divisional Cavalry Went To XIV Corps. 5.16 "B" Squadron 2nd King Edward's Horse May 1916		
Heading	War Diary Of B Squadron 2nd King Edwards Horse From 1st May 1916 To 31st May 1916		
War Diary	Grand Rullecourt	01/05/1916	30/05/1916
War Diary	Trekking	31/05/1916	31/05/1916
Miscellaneous	D.A.G. 3rd Echelon	05/06/1916	05/06/1916

WO 95/2940/1

56TH DIVISION

'B' SQDN 2ND KING ED'S HORSE
MAR - MAY 1916

To 14 CORPS

56th Divisional Cavalry.

"B" SQUADRON

2nd KING EDWARD'S HORSE

21st to 31st MARCH 1916.

WAR DIARY
or
INTELLIGENCE SUMMARY

Army Form C. 2118.

B. Squadron: 2nd K.E.H
Divisional Cavalry
5th Division

(Erase heading not required.)

Place	Date	Hour	Summary of Events and Information	Remarks and references to Appendices
	21.3.16		Left Blancacques at 10 a.m.; met "A" Squadron on the Wizerne - Fauquembergues road and were relieved by O.C. 2nd K.E.H. 21 Col: M⁰ Gadot & C⁰; proceeded from Fauquembergues to Fruges from where we Sent'd where we remained overnight. H. Seule rejoined by 3 A.S.C. drivers from Divisional Train with wagons & horses.	Nil
	22.3.16		Left Denlis at 8 a.m. for Croisette, the route being via Fruges, Crépy, Avern, St Pol, Croisette, remained at latter place overnight. Sergt. Seale was admitted to hospital, suffering from contusion over eye as the result of being kicked by a horse.	Nil
	23.3.16		Left Croisette at 7 am for Grand Rullecourt via Frevent. Rebreuvette reconnd. Arrived at Grand Rullecourt at 11 am: O.C. Squadron reporting arrival to H.Q.	Nil
Grand Rullecourt	24.3.16		Snowing all day; watering order. N⁰ 1553 Tpr McKewitt admitted to hospital.	Nil
"	25.3.16		Snow continued; watering order. N⁰ 1541 Tpr Sweeney & N⁰ 30 Tpr Jamieson admitted to hospital. (Fractured thigh - kicked by a horse)	Nil
"	26.3.16		Snowing, watering order.	Nil
"	27.3.16		Morning Parade - Inspection of horses by Veterinary Officer. Noon Parade - Officer's patrols. A.S.C. Drivers Bullock admitted to hospital.	Nil
"	28.3.16		Road Reconnaissances of Divisional area under hoof. Lectures to men	Nil

Army Form C. 2118.

WAR DIARY
or
INTELLIGENCE SUMMARY
(Erase heading not required.)

"B" Squadron; 2nd R.V.H.
Divisional Cavalry
56th Division

Place	Date	Hour	Summary of Events and Information	Remarks and references to Appendices
Grand Rullecourt	28.3.16		Instructions from H.Q.	Nil.
"	29.3.16		Same as previous day	Nil.
"	30.3.16		General fatigues, cleaning of stables, billets & camp. A.S.C. Driver Bullock discharged from hospital.	Nil.
"	31.3.16		Corps Commander Sir L. Kerr K.C.B. inspected the Squadron in the morning. Squadron parade in the afternoon. Sergt. Keats No. 1044 returned to duty from hospital. Troop No. 2, under 2nd Lieut. Lynch Staunton departed for one months training with Indian Cavalry.	Nil.

D.C. Alma Cr.
L.t.C. "B" Squadron
R.E.H.

2449 Wt. W14957/M90 750,000 1/16 J.B.C. & A. Forms/C.2118/12.

56th Divisional Cavalry

"B" SQUADRON

2nd KING EDWARD'S HORSE.

APRIL 1916.

Army Form C. 2118.

WAR DIARY
or
INTELLIGENCE SUMMARY

(Erase heading not required.)

"B" Squadron. 2nd K.E.H.
Divisional Cavalry
56th Division

Instructions regarding War Diaries and Intelligence Summaries are contained in F.S. Regs., Part II. and the Staff Manual respectively. Title Pages will be prepared in manuscript.

Place	Date	Hour	Summary of Events and Information	Remarks and references to Appendices
Camp Rubecourt	1.4.16		Squadron Parade.	Red
	2.4.16		Church Parade : 2nd Lieut. G. Heasman took over pro tem duties of A.P.M.	Red
	3.4.16		Officer's Patrols. No. 1098 Tpr Granger admitted to hospital.	Red
	4.4.16		Officer's Patrols.	Red
	5.4.16		Watering order : No. 1098 Tpr Granger discharged from hospital.	Red
	6.4.16		Squadron Parade.	Red
	7.4.16		Watering order & Hotchkiss practice. No. 1275 Tpr Baldock admitted to hospital. No. 1553 Tpr Hakewill discharged from hospital.	Red
	8.4.16		Squadron Parade.	Red
	9.4.16		Church Parade. Cycling Scouts from London Scottish attached for instruction. Reconnaissance. Lieut Long. No. 1594 Sergt. Watthew. No. 1267 Tpr Brown & No. 1418 Tpr Marsh left for Carieux for instruction in Hotchkiss Machine Gun. No. 915 Tpr Gully admitted to hospital. No. 1275 Tpr Baldock discharged from hospital.	Red
	10.4.16		Squadron Parade ; 1800 Tpr J. Peregrine arrived from the base & took on strength	Red

Army Form C. 2118.

B Squadron: 2nd N.Z.H
6) invisional Cavalry
56th Division

WAR DIARY
or
INTELLIGENCE SUMMARY
(Erase heading not required.)

Place	Date	Hour	Summary of Events and Information	Remarks and references to Appendices
Grand Rullecourt	11.4.16		Squadron Parade; No 40 Tpr Burbridge admitted to hospital	Nil
	12.4.16		Watering order & bathing parade. Leave of absence granted to the following officers & men for the periods shown :- Lieut. H.E. Osborn 13.4.16 to 21.4.16 136 Tpr Harris; 13.4.16 to 20.4.16 1263 " Dinnock; 13.4.16 to 20.4.16 1262 " Kiley; 13.4.16 to 20.4.16 1221 " Chandler; 13.4.16 to 20.4.16 7836 " Wilsdon (S.S. A.S.C.) 13.4.16 to 20.4.16 1277 " Grierson 13.4.16 to 21.4.16	On arrival at Boulogne these six men went return to unit. Leave having been postponed. Nil
	13.4.16		Watering order.	Nil
	14.4.16		Watering order & lecture on Divisional Cavalry work by Squadron Commander. Officers & men granted leave as per minute of 12.4.16, ordered to return on 18.4.16.	Nil
	15.4.16		Squadron Parade. Lieut. Heagman returned to duty.	Nil
	16.4.16		Church Parade. 6 Cycling Scouts London Scottish departed to rejoin unit.	Nil
	17.4.16		Watering order. Field day for Officers under Lt. Col. Cheyne (Indian Cavalry) No 40 Trooper Burbridge R.H. discharged from hospital.	Nil

Army Form C. 2118.

"B" Squadron
2nd R.H.
Devon Cavalry, 8th Div.

WAR DIARY
or
INTELLIGENCE SUMMARY

(Erase heading not required.)

Instructions regarding War Diaries and Intelligence Summaries are contained in F. S. Regs., Part II and the Staff Manual respectively. Title Pages will be prepared in manuscript.

Place	Date	Hour	Summary of Events and Information	Remarks and references to Appendices
Grand Rullecourt	18.4.16		Watering order. Field day for Officers, N.C.O.s under Lt. Col. Cheyne. Lt. Long, 15994 Sergt. Waltham, 1267 Tpr Moon, 1418 Tpr Knapp returned from Machine Gun course.	Nil.
	19.4.16		Watering order. Field day for Officers, N.C.O.s under Lt. Col. Cheyne. 916 Tpr Lully discharged from hospital.	Nil.
	20.4.16		Watering order. Field day for Officers, N.C.O.s under Lt. Col. Cheyne. Lt. Col. Cheyne attached to squadron.	Nil.
	21.4.16		Watering order. Field day for Officers, N.C.O.s under Lt. Col. Cheyne. Capt. Lawrence departed to take up special duty with Intelligence VI Corps.	Nil.
	22.4.16		Watering order.	Nil.
	23.4.16		Church Parade.	Nil.
	24.4.16		Watering order. Field day for Officers & N.C.O.s under Lt. Col. Cheyne. Baking Parade.	Nil.
	25.4.16		Watering order. Field day for Officers, N.C.O.s under Lt. Col. Cheyne.	Nil.
	26.4.16		Squadron Field day under Lt. Col. Cheyne.	Nil.

WAR DIARY
or
INTELLIGENCE SUMMARY
(Erase heading not required.)

Army Form C. 2118.

B' Squadron
2nd R8 N
Div: Cavalry; 56th Div.

Place	Date	Hour	Summary of Events and Information	Remarks and references to Appendices
Grand Rullecourt	27.4.16		Watering order. Field day for Officers & N.C.O's under Lt. Col Cheyne. Lt. Col Cheyne departed.	Ned.
	28.4.16		Watering order. Field day for Officers, N.C.O's under Lt. Col Cheyne. 1242 Tpr Williams J admitted to hospital.	Ned.
	29.4.16		Watering order. Nos 3 & 4 Troops. No 1 Troop Field day with London Scottish B?. Leave of absence granted to the following Officers & men for periods shown:- Lt. Long 30-4-16 to 8-5-16. 136 Tpr Harvey 30-4-16 7-5-16. 7836 " Hilsdon 30-4-16 7-5-16 (Shoeing Smith A.S.C)	Ned. Ned.
	30.4.16		Church Parade.	

D.G. Cheyne Lt.
for O.C. "B" Squadron
2RSH.

M 67

D.A.G.
3rd Echelon

I am in receipt of a communication from Divisional H.Q's to the effect that the War Diaries of my unit for February and March have not been received by you.

I beg to enclose herewith the following:-
War diary from 21-3-16 to 31-3-16
 "   "   "   1-4-16 to 30-4-16.

This covers the period my Squadron has been acting independently of the regiment. (2nd K.E.H)

Andrew W. Kelly
Major
O.C. "B" Squadron
2nd K.E.H
Divisional Cavalry

1/5/16.

56th Divisional Cavalry

Went to XIV Corps - .5.16.

"B" SQUADRON

2nd KING EDWARD'S HORSE

M A Y 1916.

Confidential

War Diary

of

B Squadron 2nd King Edwards Horse

From 1st May 1916 to 31st May 1916.

WAR DIARY
or
INTELLIGENCE SUMMARY

(Erase heading not required.)

Army Form C. 2118.

"B" Squadron
2nd King Edward's Horse

Instructions regarding War Diaries and Intelligence Summaries are contained in F. S. Regs., Part II. and the Staff Manual respectively. Title Pages will be prepared in manuscript.

Place	Date	Hour	Summary of Events and Information	Remarks and references to Appendices
GRAND RULLECOURT	1/5/16		Field day for Officers & Senior N.C.O.s under Lt. Col. Cheyne. Watering order. Leave of absence granted to the following Officers & men for the periods shown:- Lieut. Long 30.4.16 to 8.5.16 136 Tpr Harvey 30.4.16 to 7.5.16 7836 " Mitsdon 30.4.16 to 7.5.16 (Shoeing Smith - A.S.C)	
"	2/5/16		Field day for Officers & Senior N.C.O.s under Lt. Col. Cheyne. Watering order. 435 Tpr Glover 1170 Tpr Wightwick & 1762 Tpr Forbes departed on a course of signalling. No 2 Troop under 2nd Lieut. Lynch Staunton returned from one month's training with Indian Cavalry. Squadron night manoeuvres under Lt. Col. Cheyne.	
"	3/5/16		Field day for Officers & Senior N.C.O.s under Lt. Col. Cheyne. Watering order & Watering Parade. 463 Corpl. Listwood, 1362 Tpr Hungerford & 1512 Tpr Healy departed on a course of signalling.	
"	4/5/16		Field day for Officers & Senior N.C.O.s under Lt. Col. Cheyne. Watering order.	
"	5/5/16		Squadron field day under Lt. Col. Cheyne.	
"	6/5/16		Field day for Officers & Senior N.C.Os under Lt. Col. Cheyne. 2nd Lieut. Lynch Staunton, 1221 Tpr Chandler & 1262 Tpr Kilsey granted leave 6-5-16 to 13-5-16. Watering order.	
"	8/5/16		Field day for Officers & Senior N.C.O.s under Lt. Col. Cheyne. Watering order.	

Army Form C. 2118.

WAR DIARY
or
INTELLIGENCE SUMMARY

(Erase heading not required.)

"B" Squadron
2nd King Edwards Horse

Instructions regarding War Diaries and Intelligence Summaries are contained in F. S. Regs., Part II. and the Staff Manual respectively. Title Pages will be prepared in manuscript.

Place	Date	Hour	Summary of Events and Information	Remarks and references to Appendices
GRAND RULLECOURT	8/5/16		No Church Parade owing to Inspection Division moving.	
"	9/5/16		Field Day for Officers & N.C.O.s under Lt. Col. Cheyne	
"	10/5/16		Marching order. Leave granted to the following men for period shown :- 1263 Tpr Garrott 12-5-16 to 19-5-16 1277 " Ericsson 12-5-16 to 20-5-16 1297 " Clancy 12-5-16 to 20-5-16 Lt. Long & 136 Tpr Harvey & 7836 Tpr. Wilsdon rejoined from leave.	
"	11/5/16		Squadron Field Day under Lt. Col. Cheyne.	
"	12/5/16		Field day for Officers & Senior N.C.O.s under Lt. Col. Cheyne. Major R. Kelly, 2nd Lieut. Measor & 1328 Tpr Kirkward granted leave 14-5-16 to 24-5-16	
"	13/5/16		Officers & Senior N.C.O.s completed one months instruction under Lt. Col. Cheyne. Leave of absence granted to the following men for periods shown :- 1336 Tpr Borno 16-5-16 to 23-5-16 1380 " Garrett 16-5-16 to 26-5-19 1397 " Siddall 16-5-16 to 23-5-16	
"	14/5/16		443 Cpl Lidwell, 1362 Tpr Hungerford, 9/512 Tpr Healy returned from course of instruction. 2nd Lieut. Lynch & Shernden rejoined from leave. 1263 Tpr Wilkinson returned from hospital.	

WAR DIARY
or
INTELLIGENCE SUMMARY

Army Form C. 2118.

B Squadron
2nd King Edward's Horse

Place	Date	Hour	Summary of Events and Information	Remarks and references to Appendices
GRAND RULLECOURT	15/5/16		Squadron field day postponed on account of Ireland weather. 1221 Tpr Chandler & 1262 Tpr Kilsey rejoined from leave. 435 Tpr Glover 1170 Tpr Wilkinson & 1762 Tpr Forbes rejoined from course of signaling.	Nil
"	16/5/16		Squadron field day, road practice & manoeuvres.	Nil
"	17/5/16		do. do.	Nil
"	18/5/16		Watering order & grazing. 1242 Tpr Williams admitted to hospital.	Nil
"	19/5/16		Squadron field day.	Nil
"	20/5/16		Watering order & grazing.	Nil
"	21/5/16		Tpr Sixsmith (No 1263) rejoined from leave.	Nil
"	22/5/16		1277 Tpr Grierson & 1307 Tpr Clancy rejoined from leave. Squadron field day.	Nil
"	23/5/16		Watering order & grazing.	Nil
"	24/5/16		Watering order & grazing. Inspection of horses by V.O. 1611 Tpr De Roac admitted to hospital.	Nil
"	25/5/16		Squadron field day.	Nil

Army Form C. 2118.

WAR DIARY
or
INTELLIGENCE SUMMARY
(Erase heading not required.)

"B" Squadron
2nd King Edward's Horse

Place	Date	Hour	Summary of Events and Information	Remarks and references to Appendices
RAND BILLECOURT	26/5/16		Squadron Field day. 1464 Tpr Towey granted leave 26.5.16/5 3.5.16. 1336 Tpr Rowe. 1397 Tpr Siddall & 1380 Tpr Garrell rejoined from leave. 1242 Tpl Williams rejoined from hospital.	
"	27/5/16		Watering order. 1404 Tpr Knox granted leave 27-5-16/5.6.16. Major A. M. Kelso Kelly 1228 Tpr Kirkland rejoined from leave.	
"	28/5/16		Church Parade. 1210 Tpr Gallon granted leave 28.5.16 to 4.6.16.	
"	29/5/16		Horse Exercise. Watering order. 1594 R.N. Sergt Matthew granted leave 29/5/16 5/6/16	
"	30/5/16		Squadron received orders to join 2nd Army at PROVEN (BELGIUM). Squadron reached NUNCQ at 5pm where Pte Kirk 1420 5/16 to 6/4/16 GRAND ROLLECOURT at 11.30.am reaching NUNCQ at Squadron remained overnight. 917 S.S. Cpl. Williams granted leave 1601 Tpr De Roux rejoined from hospital	
TREKKING	31/5/16		Left NUNCQ at 8.45 am. reaching LILLIERS at 5.30 pm's residences night. 1384 Tpr Hancock granted leave 31.5.16 7.6.16. 1339 Tpr Linton Hough transferred to A Squadron.	

4. June 1916.—

Aylesmore. Lt.
R.T. Major
O/C "B" Squadron
2nd K.E. Edward's Horse

Q 4.

D.A.G 3rd Echelon

Herewith enclosed please find:

War diary from 1.5.16 to 31.5.16.

The delay in forwarding this is on account of my squadron having been transferred from the 56th Division to the XIV Corps.

Au O Kelly
Major
O.C. B Squadron
2nd King Edward's Horse

In the field
5/6/16.—

www.ingramcontent.com/pod-product-compliance
Lightning Source LLC
Chambersburg PA
CBHW081509160426
43193CB00014B/2631